Yoga for Cats

Traudl & Walter Reiner

YOGA FOR CATS

LONDON
VICTOR GOLLANCZ LTD
1992

For Friski, Boots
Jackie and Jed

First published in Great Britain August 1991
by Victor Gollancz Ltd
14 Henrietta Street, London WC2E 8QJ
Sixth impression February 1992

Copyright © 1990 by Traudl & Walter Reiner

A catalogue record for this book is
available from the British Library

0 575 05122 1

Printed in Italy by New Interlitho SpA, Milan

"The regular practice of asanas, pranayama and meditation will lead you to become a sleek, fulfilled and wise cat."

– Swami Pussananda

Felix

May Ling

Scrappy

Sir Henry

We thank the Board of the Yoga-Cat
Institute for its friendly support.

Whiskers   Blackie

WARM-UPS AND PRE-EXERCISES

First, relax the paws and legs. Then follow with
the belly and chest, the neck, the face
and finally with the whiskers.

Eye Movement Number One

Sit in a relaxed position. Keep your head still while following a moving object back and forth. Only your eyes should move.

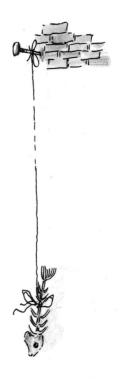

SARVANGASANA

(Shoulder Stand)

Variation
(Bridge Pose)

SIRSASANA

(Head Stand)

coming into the pose

full headstand

with legs outstretched

Lotus variation

Felix refreshes himself with a cold shower after his headstand
while Scrappy relaxes with comics.

Viparita Karani

(Upside-down Pose)

HANUMANASANA

*(Splits,
or Hanuman Pose)*

HALASANA

(Plough Pose)

Steps

BHUJANGASANA

(Cobra Pose)

Variations

SALABHASANA

(Locust Pose)

Half Locust

Full Locust

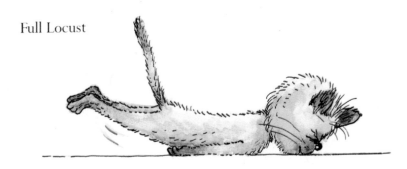

DHANURASANA

(Bow Pose)

ARDHA MATSYENDRASANA

(Half-spinal twist)

(Named after the
renowned
Yoga-master
Matsyendra)

Steps

Bent leg variation with paws
clasped behind back

full spinal twist

MAYURASANA

(Peacock Pose)

Steps

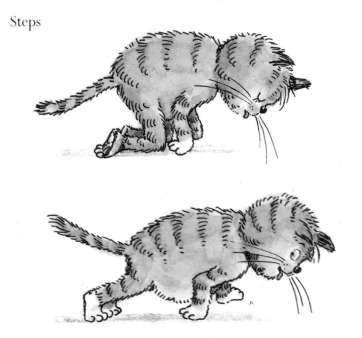

Supta Vajrasana

(Recumbent Thunderbolt Pose)

Steps

JANU SIRSASANA

(Head-to-Knee Pose)

Steps

May Ling recovers after the Janu Sirsasana
exercise with meditation music.

CHAKRASANA

(Wheel Pose)

Steps

KURMASANA

(Tortoise Pose)

Steps

CHATURKONASANA

(Four-Cornered Pose)

Variation

AKARNA DHANURASANA

(Shooting Bow Pose)

Step

Warm-Up

SAMKATASANA

(Heroic Pose)

Steps

MANDUKASANA

(Frog Pose)

Dynamic Variation

KUTILANGASANA

(Snake Pose)

SETUASANA

(Full Bridge Pose)

UTTAN PRISTHASANA

(Dog Pose)

SIMHASANA

(Lion Pose)

Variations

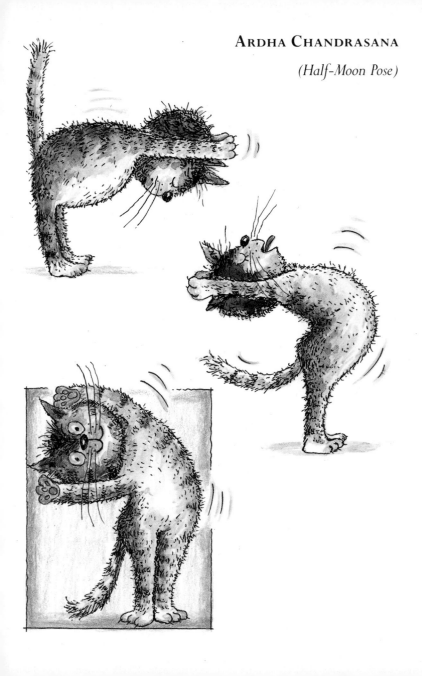

Sir Henry enjoys the break with his favourite reading.

GARUDASANA

(Eagle Pose)

Steps

VRKSASANA

(Tree Pose)

Variation   Warm-Up

NATARAJASANA

(Lord of the Dance Pose)

Steps

Variations

TRIKONASANA

(Triangle Pose)

Steps

Dynamic Variations

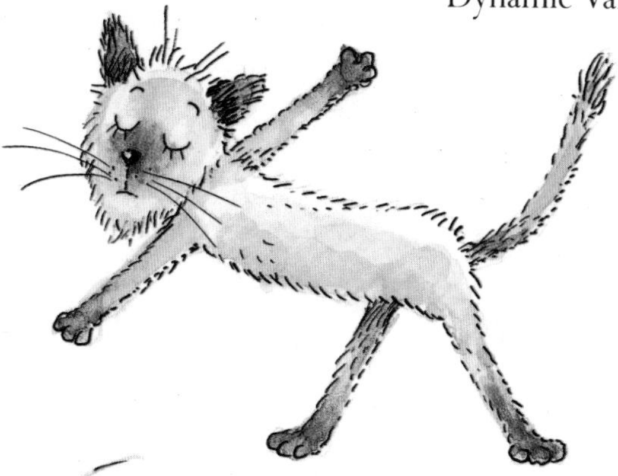

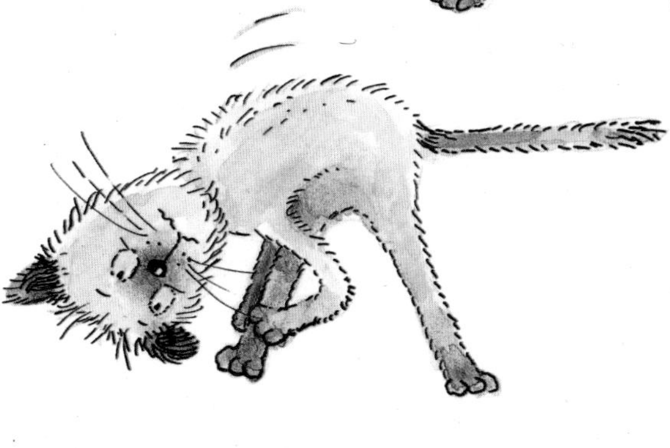

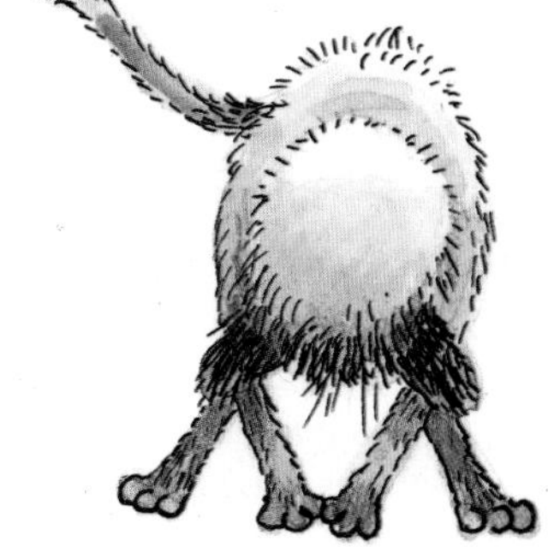

UTKATASANA

(Chair Pose)

BHADRASANA

(Gentle Pose)

SAVASANA

(Play Dead Pose)

Steps

(Full Lotus Pose)

Vajrasana
(Thunderbolt Pose)

Virasana
(Warrior Pose)

Sukhasana
(Relaxed Pose)

PADMASANA

(Lotus Position)

Warm-Ups

Blackie takes a break from training and relaxes with the 'mouse programme'.

1. Variation

2. Variation

PADMASANA

(Lotus Position)

3. Variation

Yoga Mudra

(Tied and Bound Pose)

Steps

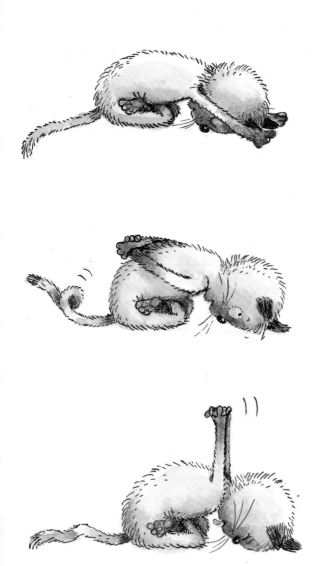

SURYANAMASKAR

(Sun Salute)

1 →

1 →

1 →

Whiskers' 'Sun Salute' during the break from training.

UDDIYANA BANDHA

(Stomach Hold)

Steps

Maha Bandha

*(Great Lock or
Chin Lock)*

Steps

MAHA VEDA

(Rooster Pose)

Variation

BREATHE DEEPLY

Warm-Ups

Press the diaphragm forward
and let the belly expand.

Exhale, draw in the diaphragm
and let the belly contract.

PRANAYAMA

*(Breathing
Practices)*

Steps

Alternate nostril breathing.